Safari Dreaming

AN AFRICAN EXPERIENCE IN THE SOUTH LUANGWA VALLEY, ZAMBIA.

Photography by Paul Joynson-Hicks

blue mango publishing

All black and white prints are a variety of specialist toned silver gelatin prints done by Debbie Sears at Metro Imaging in London, UK - www.metroimaging.co.uk

Acknowledgements

I am deeply grateful to Robin and Jo Pope who put me up in their camps and to Jo for her inspiration and vision. Naturally, as the saying goes, without them none of this would have been possible. To Robin, many thanks for being 'the Reluctant Hero'! Robin Pope Safaris have a fantastic team and I would love to thank you all for being so warm and welcoming. You are indubitably the most disreputable bunch of glorious bush fiends and I love you all - it was you lot who made putting this book together so much fun.

The book consists of both colour and black and white pictures and I would like to thank Debbie Sears and Metro Imaging in London for giving me such brilliant prints. Debbs, you're a genius. For my equipment surviving the grueling toils of the bush on endless trips my thanks go to Gray Levett at Grays of Westminster and Nikon for such brilliant kit.

Completing this book has been great fun, although sometimes it must have been very frustrating for the excellent designer, Ronelle Pitzer at Grey Zone. Ron thanks for such wonderful and inspired work under such nightmare conditions. The book reproduction and much organisation was done by Les Martens at Unifoto International in Cape Town; huge thanks to Les for being so tolerant and efficient. For proofing, editing and endless helpful hints many thanks to Louisa Muir and Marcus Prior. For kind hospitality in Cape Town many thanks to Marcus again and Paddy Radcliffe.

My special thanks to Jenny and David Rossi, Tony Keene, Julia Cassels, Jackie Erickson and Mani Holmes, all brilliant artists who left their beautiful sketches in the visitors books which I have purloined and used in the introductions. Thanks guys, you are all wonderfully gifted!

Finally, as you all breathe a sigh of relief, I must thank my gorgeous wife, Helen. Thank you so much for putting up with my absences. I couldn't have done it without you.

Please note: all the photography here is totally organic! No visually altering filters or digital manipulation has been used.

First published by Blue Mango Publishing 2002
P.O. Box 70045
Dar es Salaam
Tanzania

ISBN 9987 - 8934 - 1 - 4

Designed by Grey Zone Productions
Colour reproduction by Unifoto International, Cape Town.
Printed by Tieh Wah Press, Singapore.

CONTENTS

Photograher's Note

Safari Dreaming is a glimpse into the breathtaking world of a safari in Africa, and here in particular as guests of Robin Pope Safaris in Zambia's South Luangwa National Park. It is by no means a comprehensive guide to either the South Luangwa or to the safari experience. Purely a peek, a foretaste, a slice of what you might see and enjoy.

Working closely with Jo Pope I have compiled the book as a day on safari; dawn, midday, dusk and night. Robin Pope Safaris has three camps, Nkwali in the central area and Tena Tena and Nsefu in the northern part of the park, as well as a mobile camp. All the camps feature prominently in the pages that follow.

In order to make the pages as uncluttered as possible and to allow the pictures to speak for themselves, captions have been printed at the end of the book.

I hope that you enjoy Safari Dreaming and that if you have not yet been to Africa it may draw you here, if you have visited that it may draw you back and if you live here...thank the good Lord.

Paul Joynson-Hicks

INTRODUCTION

The Luangwa Valley, a branch of the Great Rift Valley, lies in eastern Zambia. Bordered by the steep Muchinga Escarpment in the west and rolling hills to the east, it is a wide, open valley floor of woodland, dambos and oxbow lagoons. The most spectacular feature of this remote valley is the meandering Luangwa River. A major tributary of the Zambezi, it is one of the last remaining rivers in the world that flows without man-made interference. Uninterrupted for 700 kilometers, this dynamic river snakes through one of Africa's richest wildlife areas. In 1866, Livingstone crossed the Luangwa on his third and last expedition to the interior. He wrote in his journal, "I will make this beautiful land better known to men that it may become one of their haunts. It is impossible to describe its luxuriance."

The Honey Pot

Due to its rich natural resources, the Luangwa Valley has been a honey pot for man since the Stone Age. But conditions are difficult and the seasons extreme, so man tended to raid the pot from the more hospitable surrounding plateau areas. It was not until the mid-19th

Century that any tribe settled in the area – and their descendants are still there. These are the Kunda, who migrated southwards from the Luba Empire, which then covered most of Central Africa.

Over the centuries, the Luangwa Valley has been a magnet for hunters, both local and foreign. The prolific game, in particular the elephant and hippopotamus, attracted Portuguese, Chikunda and Arab traders, and later, British trophy hunters. The excessive hunting of game continued when the territory became British in 1891. The big-game hunters and sporadic outbreaks of disease had such an effect on certain populations of wildlife that steps had to be taken to ensure their survival. The hippopotamus were protected in 1906 along certain stretches of the Luangwa River. The British administration slowly increased efforts to protect the environment, declaring game reserves within the Luangwa Valley in 1938. Only later, in 1971, did the independent Zambian government change the status of these reserves to national parks, to include the South Luangwa National Park. This protection was so successful that the teeming game populations that resulted began to degrade the environment themselves and in the 1960s culling programmes were introduced. However, within a decade the pendulum swung back the other way as a result of a massive increase in commercial poaching.

The Poaching Blitz

Over a fifteen-year period from the early 1970s, the threat from commercial poaching was considerable. The main targets were the black rhino, for their horn, and the elephants for their tusks. In the early 1970s, the Luangwa Valley was home to a strong black rhino population of around 4000. After the poaching 'blitz', the rhino population was virtually wiped out. Elephant numbers in the Luangwa Valley basin declined dramatically from 100,000 to around 12,000. The poaching decreased from the late 1980s as the market for ivory declined and various internationally sponsored wildlife management bodies were put in place. Presently, the elephant population is slowly increasing again.

As in any wilderness area, the wildlife population of the Luangwa Valley is susceptible to the influence of man. Commercial poaching continues to be a problem but the snaring of animals for meat is possibly a greater threat today. But where man lives alongside wildlife, there

will always be conflict. Certain species are vulnerable to epidemics of disease or environmental cycles. The anthrax outbreak of 1987 drastically affected the wild dog population, but the species is now thought to be turning the corner and increasing in numbers again after ten years of decline. The Cookson's wildebeest, one of two endemic species, is presently declining in numbers, possibly due to human encroachment outside the National Park and overshooting. However, most wildlife populations are exceptionally healthy. The Thornicroft giraffe, the second endemic species to the Luangwa, is presently at a population of around 500 and probably increasing, though at the turn of the century trophy hunting had virtually wiped out this species. The Luangwa River has one of the highest hippopotamus densities in Africa and leopard sightings continue to be exceptionally high for any wildlife area.

Photographic Safaris

Photographic safaris started as early as 1950 with the opening of Nsefu Camp, a partnership between the Game Department and the local chief. The concept of local communities benefiting directly from tourism is considered a recent progressive development in Africa but the practice was in place long ago in the Luangwa Valley. The visionary Norman Carr was intimately involved from an early stage and later, when he retired from the department as a game ranger in 1961, he introduced the concept of "walking safaris" for tourists traveling with their cameras. Today, the Luangwa Valley is renowned as probably the premier walking safari area in Africa.

Robin and Jo Pope

Norman Carr developed a number of camps in the South Luangwa National Park area and it is at one of these that Robin Pope joined him as a young safari guide. Born in 1951, Robin spent his boyhood running around in the bush with his pellet gun and fishing rod. His family spent many holidays in different parts of Zambia, including the Luangwa Valley, and by the time he reached adulthood his knowledge and understanding of the bush was extensive. In 1976, after working in the Lower Zambezi as a field officer for an exploration company

and later for Wildlife Conservation International, the opportunity to work as a safari guide in the Luangwa arose. He packed his bush kit into his prized Landrover and headed eastwards. He has lived and worked in the Luangwa Valley ever since.

Robin guided for Norman for five years and then managed Nsefu Camp for a further five years. It was during his time at Nsefu that his international reputation developed. In 1986 Robin started out on his own with the opening of Tena Tena Camp. Two years later Jo arrived from England. She had read zoology at university, worked in the restaurant and film industries and was well traveled. With her came business acumen, as well as a love of the bush, to enhance Robin's skills and dreams. Together they built up Robin Pope Safaris. They opened Nkwali Camp in 1991 and later reopened Nsefu Camp in 1999. They also operate the best known walking safaris in Zambia, using a totally mobile camp. As one journalist put it.....

"Their camps take, at most, a dozen pampered visitors, everyone of whom is treated as a personal house guest and new best friend. The Popes have set a standard that has become Zambia's benchmark for excellence and their guides are astonishingly knowledgeable naturalists."

Artwork: Robin Pope

The ethos of Robin Pope Safaris is simple. They aim to give their guests a chance to experience the magical side of the bush in its entirety, and so enhance the guest's awareness of nature. The 'experience' of a safari with Robin and Jo, and their team, touches you at a deep level. "It's a soul thing".

Muchinga Escarpment
Mupamadzi River
To LUNDAZI
N
Walking mobile area
Nsefu Trails walking camp
Nsefu
Tena Tena
Nkwali
To CHIPATA
MFUWE AIRPORT
Luangwa River
To PETAUKE
0 10 20 Km
SOUTH LUANGWA NATIONAL PARK

DAWN

...crisp clear air, ...silver and red tinged clouds, ...the rustle of wings as

knob-billed duck power over in formation, ...the dispersal call of a hyena,

...smell of woodsmoke, ...the night still clinging to the trees, ...the tree tops,

...slowly emerging tinged with gold, ...a thousand quelia rustling their wings,

...taste of fresh tea brewed on the open fire, ...the tropical boubou calling from

a nearby bush, ...the flood of light down the river, ...hot toast from the mopane

coals, ...the golden light slanting through the ebony grove

baboons barking at the leopard...

Many thanks to you all
Mani.

Jenny & David Rossi.
15th June 2001.

MIDDAY

...the harsh strong light overhead, ...deep shadows under the trees, ...zebra tentatively crossing the sand bank to drink, ...dust devils swirling across the sand, ...elephants mud bathing, ...raptors soaring high in the sky, ...vultures circling over last night's kill, ...hippos snoozing on the sand, ...puku out in the sun, ...elephants sleeping on termite mounds, ... warthogs in mud, ...lions shading under the bushes...

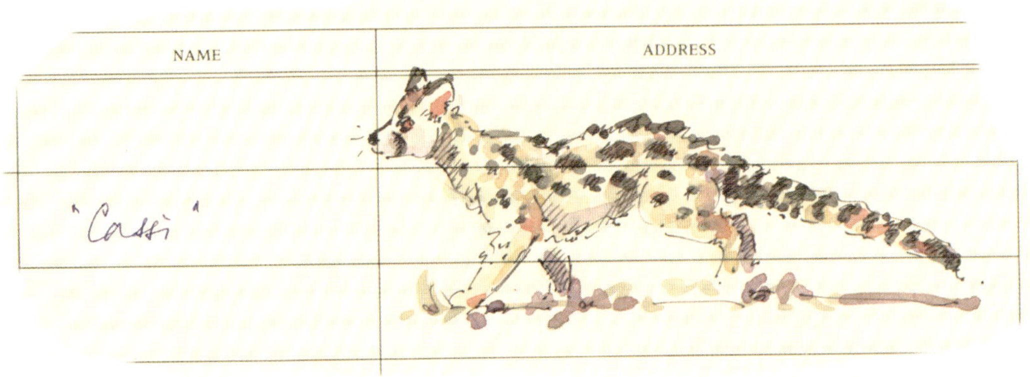

DUSK

...heat of the day fading, ...guinea fowl flying to the ebony trees to roost, ...carmine bee-eaters swooping at their colony, ...hippos starting to leave the river to feed, ...sundowners on the banks of the Luangwa, ...orange and red light reflected on the water, ...silhouette of huge trees against the red sky, ...a pair of pearl spotted owlets whistling to each other, ...a thousand quelias flocking to the reeds.

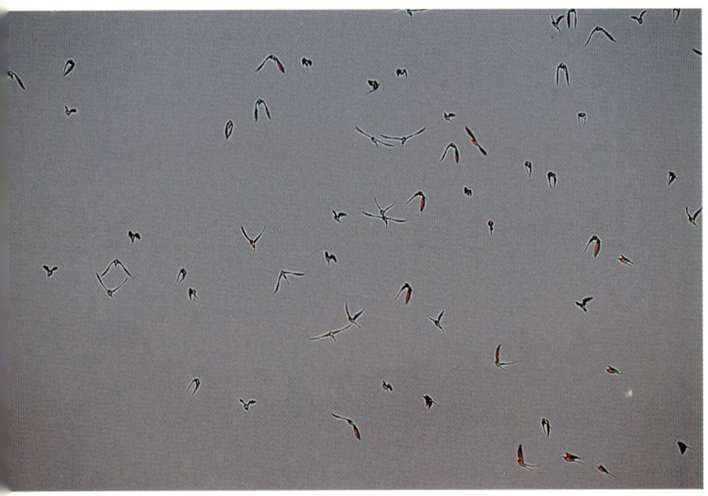

NIGHT

…moon rising, …nightjars flitting through the dark, …baboons barking at the leopard on the prowl, …civet feeding on ebony fruit, …bats supping from the sausage tree flowers, …hyaenas whooping, …anticipation of following lions hunting, …pels fishing owl calling, …sitting round the camp fire with a nightcap, …bright starlight, …unseen elephants ripping the bush as they feed, …lying in bed, very still, as lions call nearby

It's a soul thing...

KAWAZA VILLAGE

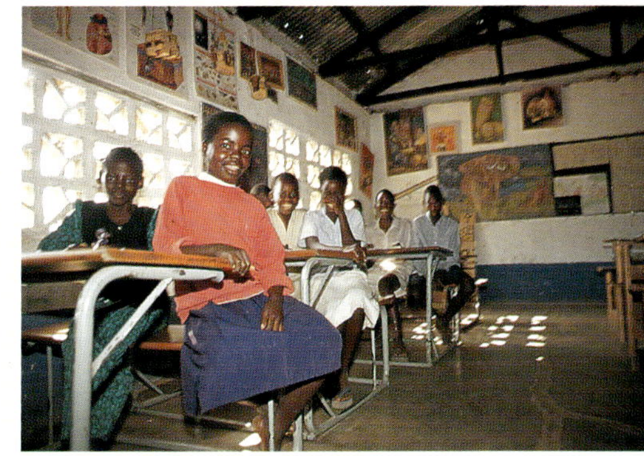

A safari in Africa goes beyond wildlife and sweeping landscapes; it is also about meeting the people. Kawaza village, with assistance from Jo Pope, has opened its doors to guests keen to spend a day with the community or even stay for a night. This exchange contributes to the support of the school, local orphans and disabled people. An innovative project, Kawaza village is a highlight of the safari.

THIS IS MY HOUSE.

IN SMALL

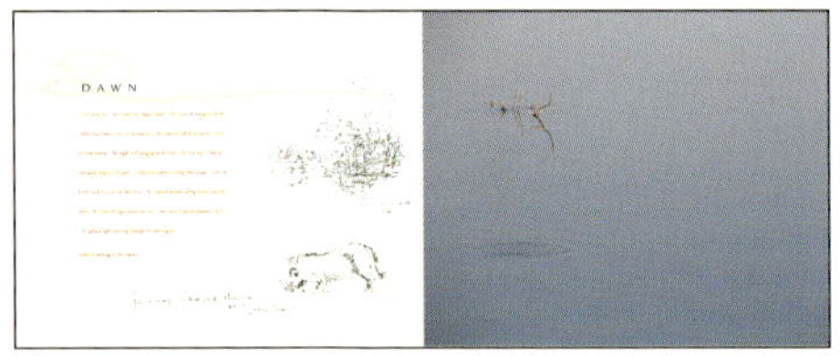

page2 Dawn over the Luangwa River.

page3 Sunrise on Chichele Salt Pan.

page4 Breakfast in the camps is always fun if you have the energy that is, at that ridiculous time of day. RPS is well known for its morning porridge in the 'three-legged pot'.

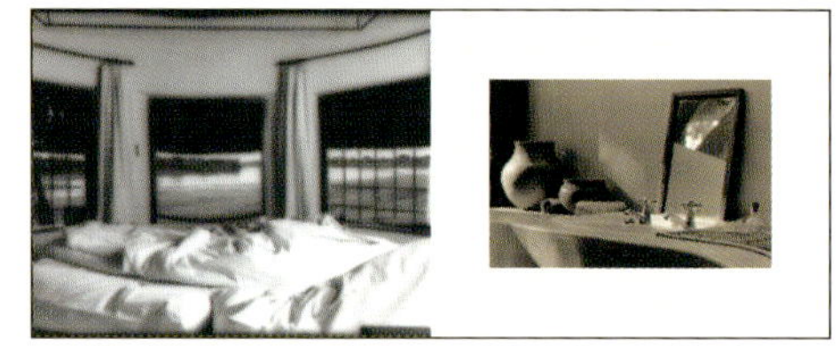

page5 Nsefu bedroom, not a view to take lightly.

page6 The bathroom at Nkwali.

page7 Leadwood tree *combretum imberbe.*

page8 Noodles stirring the famous porridge at Nsefu. The caterers are legends of note at RPS. You will get fed and watered until you can barely move!

page9 Leopard *panthera pardus* in a tamarind tree near Chembe lagoon, in Tena Tena's area.

page10 The Giant eagle owl or Verreaux or Milky *bubo lacteus.*

page11 Leopard in the same tree sunning itself.

page12 Two female puku *kobus vardonii senganus* not completely sure of whats going on here…

page13 Walking in the African bush is one of lifes great experiences and the South Luangwa has a huge variety of places to walk in. Walking here at the Manzi confluence.

page14 Baby puku, did you know that they don't give off much scent so they can hide in the grass when the folks are away feeding and not get eaten by predators!

page15 Black necked spitting cobra *naja nigricolis woodi* and in case you were wondering I am a total coward when it comes to snakes, so I shot this thing with a huge long lens so I could stand miles away!

page16 Slightly less dangerous creature and probably food for the snake but this African tree squirrel is remarkable for its inordinantly large testicles no one knows why…

page17 Young Thornicrofts giraffe *giraffa camelopardalis thornicrofti.* This sub species is unique to the South Luangwa, He's very special.

page18 A group of young male Kudu *tragelaphus strepsiceros.*

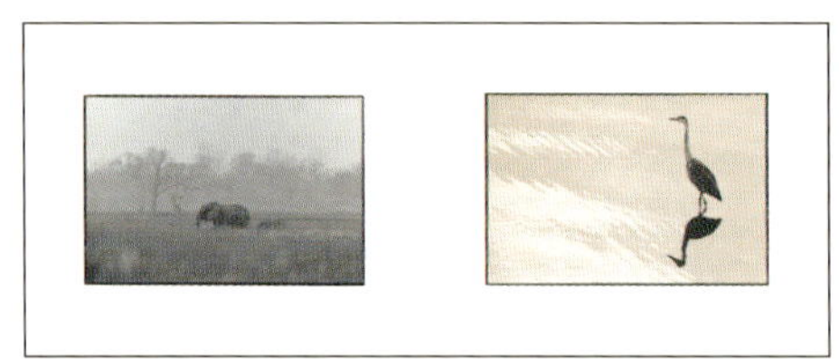

page19 Elephant mother and calf like the Chichele Pan for its salty plants and mineral deposits.

page20 Grey Heron *ardea cineara* often fish from hippos backs.

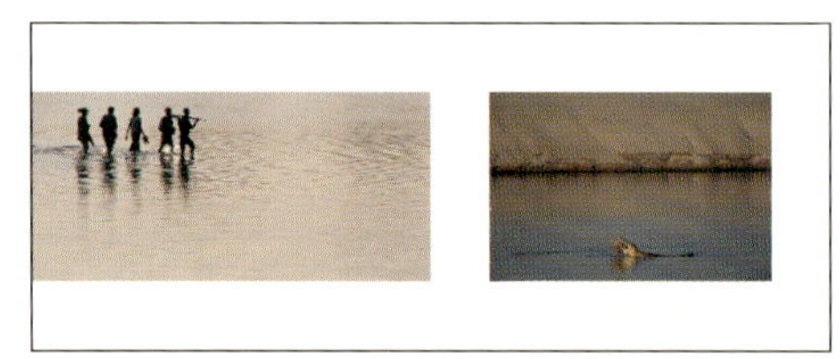

page21 You can walk anywhere in the South Luangwa, and I mean anywhere!

page22 Crocodile *crocodilus niloticus* feeding, not on those walkers I might add. Crocs can't chew, so they rip and tear and often wait for things to rot a bit so its easier to rip. Hmmm.

page23 Leopard are opportunistic hunters…

page24 Female impala *aeypceros melampus* are opportunistic escapers…

page25 Tuskless female elephant *loxodonta africana.*

page26 Lions are one of the least succesful hunters in Africa, but they mate for 2-3 days on the trot, some consolation I suppose!

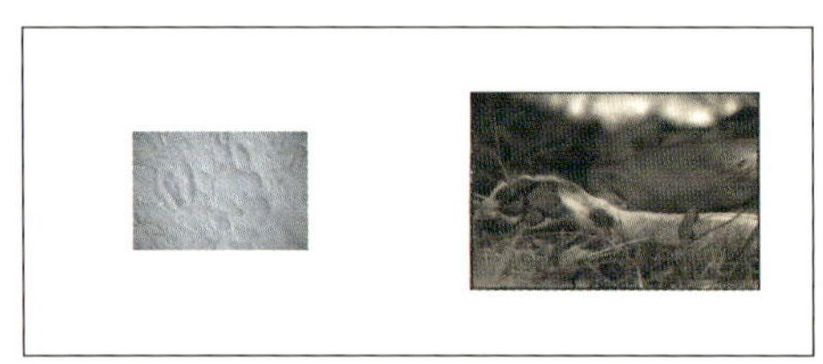

page27 I am reliably informed this is the front and rear prints of a lioness.

page28 The lioness paw with the dew claw slightly above the main paw lends extra grip whilst attacking fast moving pray.

page29 Young yellow baboon *papio cynocephales* in an ebony grove. They love eating the ebony's 'fruit of paradise'.

page30 Helmuted guinea fowl *numida meleagris* taking an early morning dust bath, which removes excess oils, parasites and probably feels great as well - sounds like an ad for Wash 'n' Go.

page31 Elephants can see movement from about 200 yards. They are very 'bush aware'.

page32 Buffalo *syncerus caffer* are one of the real dangers when walking in Africa.

page33 & 34 Elephant in the ebony groves. They love the ebony groves for the fruits of the trees and there will be good water as well. This is the first ebony grove at Tena Tena.

page35 & 36 The African wild dog *lycaon pictus*. The most beautiful, the most intelligent, the most sociable and the most effective hunters, it is tragic that they have become so endangered.

page37 The Sausage Tree *kigelia africana*. The hanging stems are called 'brats' which are much loved by elephants.

page38 The sausage tree story continues; the flowers are eaten by monkes, antelopes, porcupines and others. They are pollenated by birds and bees and by bats at night. The nectar in the petals is incredilby sweet making them very attractive food. They are around from about July through to October.

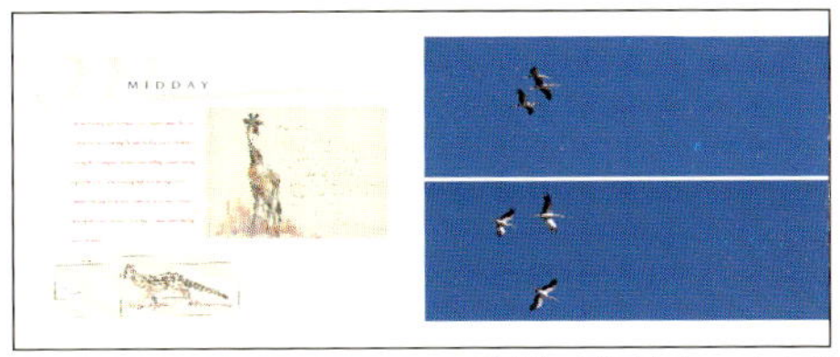

page40 Yellow billed storks *mycteria ibis*.

page41 Game driving is also great fun, and you get into the park from Nkwali either by bridge or by this pontoon.

page42 Watching a juvenile martial eagle *polemaetus bellicosus* try to extricate his claws from the monitor lizard he has caught. They were firmly stuck.

page43 & 44 Elephants having drunk at Big Bend on the Luangwa river, at Nsefu's 2nd ebony grove.

page45 Spotted bush snake *philothamnus semivariegatus*, harmless but that didn't stop one disreputable guide, Jason, from terrorising me with it when I was peacefully minding my own business.

page46 Nile monitor lizard *veranus niloticus* eat bee eater eggs and chicks and croc eggs amongst other tender morsels.

page47 Lilian's lovebirds *agapornis lilianae* only found in eastern Zambia and Malawi.

page48 More lovebirds. They are seedeaters and often found on the ground eating… wait for it… seeds.

page49 The magnificent male Greater kudu, the older the male the longer his horns and when they get really old the tips of the horns get ivory coloured.

page50 The rest of the family of female kudu. They are browsers and their stripes help to camouflage them in the bush.The females in particular are great jumpers.

page51 I say! Jolly good show! Anyone for a punt up the Luangwa…

page52 Hey, look at my teeth!

page53 The zebra in the South Luangwa are also very special, a sub species called *equus quagga crawshayi*.

page54 Crowned crane *balearica regulorum*. There is some dispute about whether it is actually crowned or crested as a crest moves up and down and a crown doesn't - but you can see it is down when flying…or is it just the wind…but does that matter…in fact does any of this matter?

page55 & 56 African green pidgeons *treron calva*, little bee eaters *merops pusillus*, red billed quelea *quelea quelea*, crowned or crested cranes, fish eagle *haliaeetus vocifer* calling, crested barbet *trachyphonus vaillantii*.

page57 & 58 One of the amazing spectacles you can experience in the South Luangwa. These elephants are in Chipela Cha Ndombo, which means Cha Ndombo's lagoon. No one seems to know who Ndombo was though.

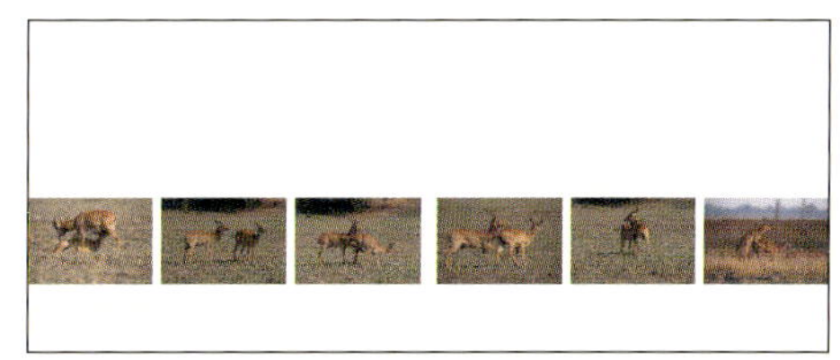

page59 & 60 Puku mating. A small note on this issue - pukus are unusual in the animal kingdom for the long duration of their foreplay.

page61 Juvenile Bateleur eagle *terathopius ecaudatus*. The young generally have a longer tail for the flight training period, as they get to grips with the flying thing the feathers fall out and a new high performance tail is revealed.

page62 I used to confuse male and female Bateleurs until a very non pc guide told me once that if you think of men being broadminded and women narrow minded (which of course I don't believe for a minute) the male Bateleur has a broad black stripe on the underside of its wing and the female a narrow one. This as you now know is a male Bateleur.

page63 Elephants often feed on trees above them and have been know to rear onto their back legs to reach higher.

page64 The marks in this footprint (this is the rear track as the front is round) are the equivalent to the crease lines in the palm of your hand, the sole of the ele foot can contract and move freely. The baby is about 6 months old, babies are weaned at about 4 years old although they will start eating solids at about 8 months.

page65 Pregnant female zebra. The Crawshay zebra has stripes right down to the hoof,as you can see here.

page66 It is difficult to tell males from females in a group except the fact that the 'stallion' is usually the last to leave.

page67 Young male kudu. The kudu are one of the 'halted' species, the halter referring to the mark on it's nose between the eyes.

page68 Baby Chobe bushbuck *tragelaphus scriptus*. You will often hear them in the bush barking to alert each other to danger.

page69 The symbiosis of the fig tree. It provides for so many creatures; the monkeys and birds in the branches let figs fall to the ground where they are then eaten by everyone from elephants to warthogs.

page70 Elephants, fig tree and Lunga Lagoon.

page71 Red billed oxpeckers *buphagas erythroryhchus* removing unwanted ticks and other bugs from dozing hippos.

page72 Crocs feeding on a dead hippo. The Luangwa River has the highest concentration of crocodiles (within the park) in Africa.

page73 Cookson's wildebeeste *conochaetes taurinus cooksoni* in the Chichele region of the park. These are also a special sub species endemic to this park.

page74 The wildebeeste and zebra are usually found in association with each other.

page75 Cookson's wildebeeste.

page76 Wild jasmine *holarrhena pubescens*. This is used for making home made gun powder, at least so say the local poachers.

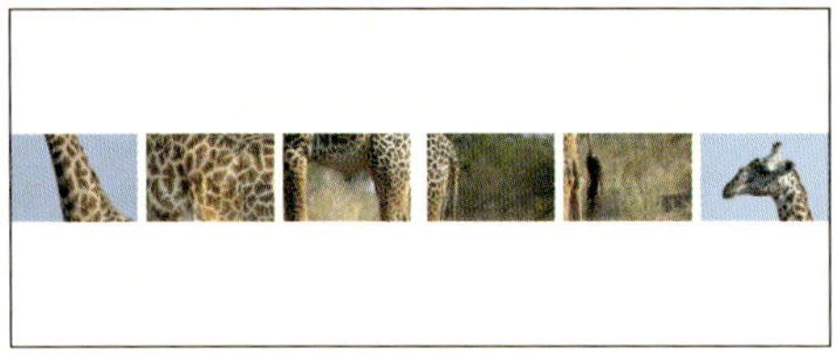

page77 & 78 Build your own Thornicrofts giraffe.

page79 & 80 The lagoons are made of plasticised laminated clays. Whatever that may be!

page81 & 82 The Fishing Party; every year near the end of the dry season the lagoons dry up and the high concentration of fish brings out a host of bird life all squabbling and feeding intensivey. This usually occurs during from July to September.

page83 Lions can mate for up to 3 days on the trot, actually mating every 15 mins or so. These guys look like they are on day three!

page84 Not everyone gets mated...

page85 Warthogs *phacochoeres aethiopicus sundavelli* love wallowing to stay cool.

page86 Piglets or 'wartlets' outside Tena Tena. A group of warthogs is called a 'sounder', bet you didn't know that!

page87 Elephants in Nsefu's first ebony grove.

page88 Lunch in the same ebony grove on a different day.

page89 Elephants crossing the Luangwa River with Nsefu behind.

page90 Old male warthog, with exceptionally large tusks.

page91 Nkwali

page92 Nkwali from the river

page93 Bird watching on a bend in the river, or at least I was until I got greatly inspired to take this picture.

page94 One of the many places you can relax and enjoy the awesome views at Nkwali.

page95 The mobile camps of RPS are in the north part of the park in the Mupamadzi area. You are in complete peace and solitude, a beautiful place to walk for a few days.

page96 The Mupamadzi river.

page97 Tena Tena bathrooms.

page98 Tent interior at Tena Tena.

page99 The food at all the camps is exceptional and much of the vegetables and fruit comes from their own garden down at Nkwali.

page100 Amazing food, very tasty and beautifully presented.

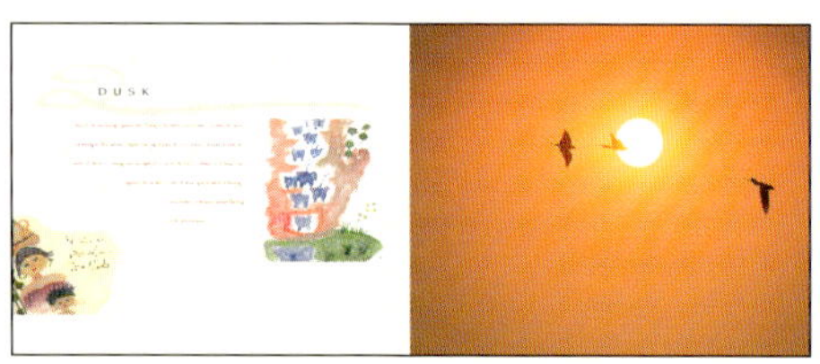

page102 Southern carmine bee eaters *merops nubicoides*.

page103 & 104 Tea at Tena Tena.

page105 The Luangwa river near Baka Baka lagoon.

page106 Up stream in the dry season, with a high hippo concentration.

page107 This is whats referred to as Extreme Walking!

page108 This is the other side of walking, peace and tranquility as the sun sets.

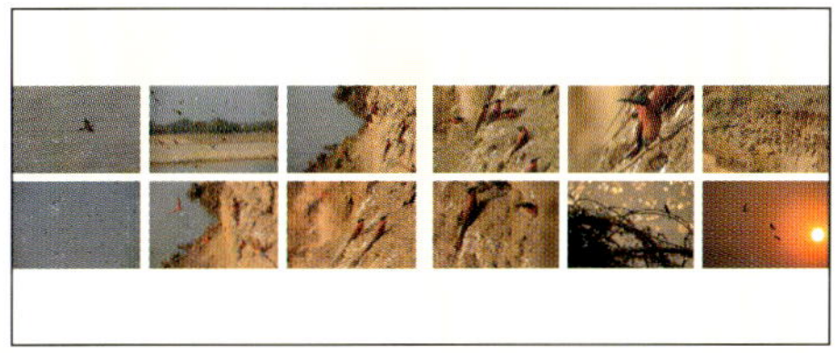

page109 & 110 Southern carmine bee eaters *merops nubicoides* make huge nesting colonies in the South Luangwa around August and September. They nest in the banks as the soil type is easy to work with and they have a safety buffer of water underneath them. Some of the nest holes can reach 2 metres inside the bank. There is even one recorded hole 7 metres deep.

page111 Blackson Zulu, wildlife scout. These are the guys with the guns when you are walking in the bushes.

page112 Leopards hunt mainly at night.

page113 & 114 The combined effect of man and wind on wild animals.

page115 Lion greetings.

page116 Lion feedings.

page117 Giant eagle owl with a genet cat in its claws.

page118 Young leopard with a beautiful ring of joined up dots on its neck, known as a 'collar'.

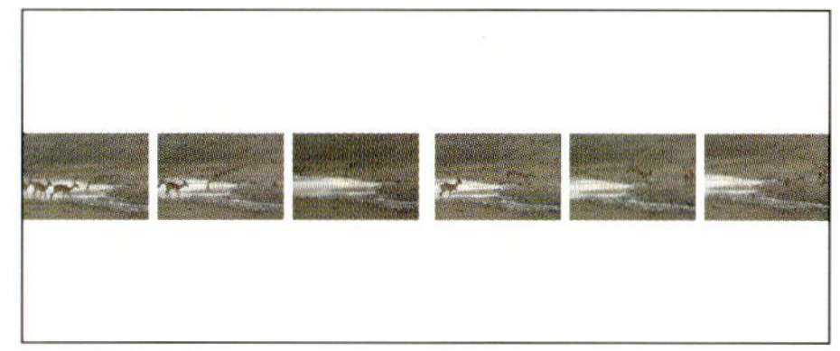

page119 & 120 Impala, well known within the animal kingdom for their superior intelligence often pointlessly jumping a very shallow stream.

page121 Lioness ready to feed.

page122 Common waterbuck *kobus ellipsyprymnus.*

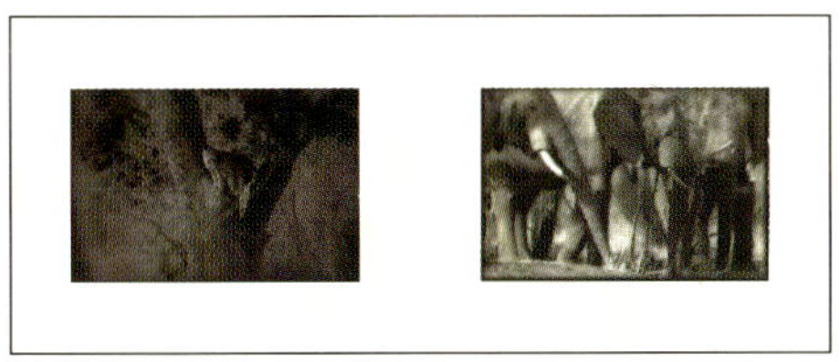

page123 Leopards often use trees as good vantage points to watch for prey or to store it away from scavangers.

page124 Murmurings of trunkcalls' .

page125 Sundowners at Tena Tena.

page126 Sundown at Nsefu.

page127 Tena Tena

page128 Alfred Sakala, wildlife scout not sure what he's doing standing in the river!

page129 *hippopotamus amphibius*

page130 Giant eagle owl.

page131 & 132 Simon, Gid, Bazz and Holty enjoying sundowners in the river.

page133 & 134 Sunset at Tena Tena.

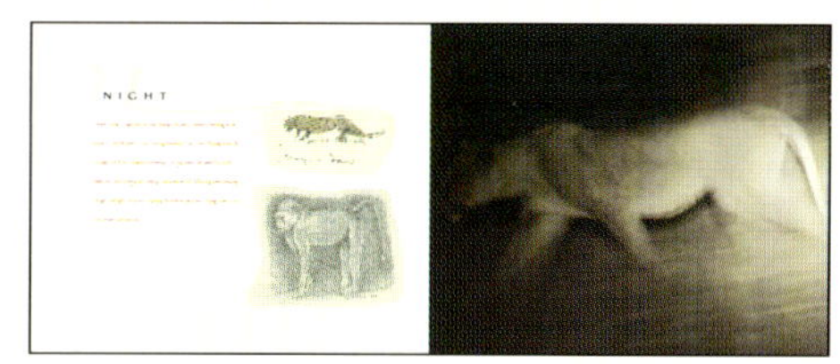

page136 The publisher asked if I was pushing the bounds of creativity too far… "Absolutely not" I replied, "elephants love hunting at night!"

page137 & 138 Dinner on the sand bank in front of Nsefu.

page139 Keyala Phiri lantern lighting.

page140 Leopards dinner.

page141 You see many animals at night, including these drooling buffalo.

page142 Bar-b-que dinner at Nkwali.

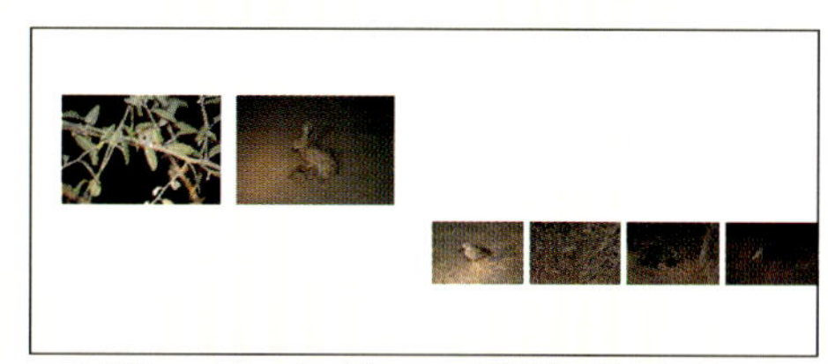

page143 Mouse of some description on a woolly caper bush *cappris tormentosa* and scrub hare.

page144 Water dikkop *burhinus vimiculatus*, four-toed elephant shrew *petrodomus tetradactylus*, civet *civettictis civeta*, white tailed mongoose *ichneumia albicauda.*

page145 Spotted hyaena *crocuta crocuta*, incidentally they are in their own scientific family *hyaenidae*.

page146 Elephant, very active at night.

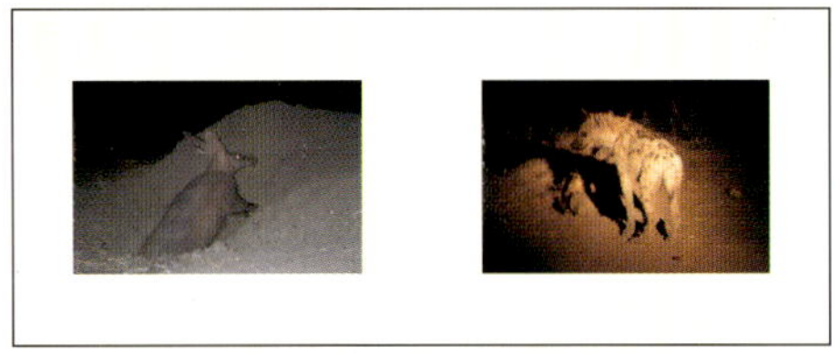

page147 The highly elusive aardvark *orycteropus afer.* It is very rare to get a photo of an aardvark and only the hardiest most resilient photographers can get one. Naturally this was got after hours and hours of waiting in the cold and wet etc... by a camera with an infrared trap while I was comfortably tucked up in bed!

page148 Hyaena. Although fantastic hunters in their own right in the South Luangwa they rarely do so as it is much easier for them to scavange from lion or leopard kills.

page149 A young male lion feeding on a puku, no Chateau Lafitte for him.

page150 Ah, the claret is for us at Nkwali.

page151 The moon.

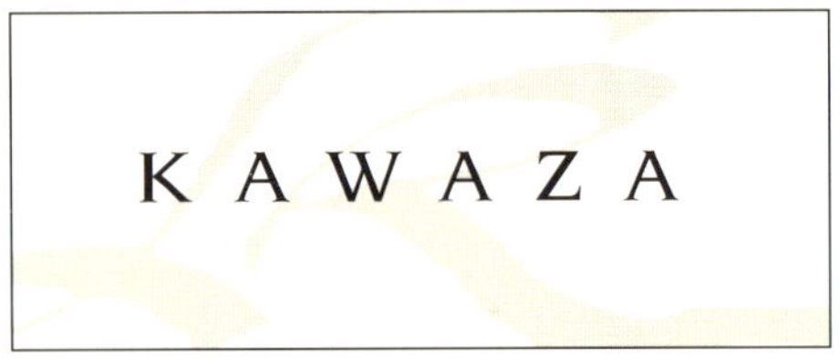

page153 & 154 Kawaza - the village project RPS supports.

page155 & 156 Kawaza - the village project RPS supports.